A Catalogue record for this book is available from the
British Library.

ISBN-13: 978-0-9562656-0-9

Typeset in Century by Paul Wilson

Printed in the UK by CPI Cox & Wyman, Reading

The paper and board used in the paperback by Caboodle
Books Ltd are natural recyclable products made from wood
grown in sustainable forests. The manufacturing processes
conform to the environmental regulations of the country of
origin.

Caboodle Books Ltd
Riversdale, 8 Rivock Avenue, Steeton, BD20 6SA
Tel: 01535 656015

By Brian Moses

Illustrations by Chris White

CABOODLE BOOKS LTD

To the pupils and staff in the
Junior Department of the
North London Collegiate School
where I have been welcomed
on many occasions.

Contents

The Great Galactic Ghoul

Don't fool around
with the great galactic ghoul,
it's not the sort of creature
to play by the rules.
For any spaceship
sent its way
will not return
to Earth someday.
It will simply bat it
out of the sky,
splat it hard
just like a fly

This ghoul was never taught
right from wrong,
it lives by its muscles,
is incredibly strong.
It's ugly as Medusa
whose snakes have just woken,
with a nose like a boxer's
that's regularly broken.
Eyes like saucers,
the flying kind,
acts like a creature
that's lost its mind.

1   poem continues...

And the gruesome great
galactic ghoul
does very little
but slobber and drool
as it shuffles about
on the edge of Mars
and anyone flying
in from the stars
should beware the ghoul,
stay clear of its lair
or it might just swing you
round by your hair.
then squeeze you between
its loathsome jaws
till it swallows you,
rubs its belly
and ROARS.

P.S.

It lives a long way away from you
and that's where it usually stays.
but something's gone wrong,
the ghoul has gone,
now it hasn't been seen for
days.........

Astronaut School

Wouldn't it be cool to go to Astronaut School,
to unravel the mysteries of space travel,
to find out what the universe is all about,
from the mathematics of rocket ships
to the science of a lunar eclipse?
Wouldn't it be brill to fill your head
with formulas for the right type of rocket fuel,
or for working out how much thrust
you must have to land safely on Mars?
Wouldn't it be great to practise
moonwalking in Games, and instead of French
learn Martian or Venusian,
knowing that someday,
when your training was done,
you might even go where they're spoken?
Wouldn't it be fab to learn about lunar habitats,
to discover what grows in dust
or what stops rust on satellites?

All in all, it's clever stuff,
far too clever for me.
I'll just stay here and dream my way
through English, Maths and PE.

The Intergalactic Holiday Bus

The Intergalactic Holiday Bus
got lost on the byways of Mars.
The driver was out of practice
at navigating by stars.
His sat nav broke and the bus took off
in completely the wrong direction
and when 'turn around' became possible
they'd missed an important connection.

They'd travelled the scenic routes
and been round places of interest.
Everyone journeying on the bus
had all been really impressed.
But they'd stopped for too many photos
and for too many trips to the loo,
and the driver's sat nav was telling them
ridiculous things to do.

Now they'd miss the mountains of Jupiter
if they waited for another ship
that would take them on to Saturn
where they could rejoin their trip.
And they'd miss the special excursion
to one of Jupiter's moons
where some overactive volcano
was sending out sulphur plumes.

Still, they'd be in time to go skating
round one of Saturn's rings
then onto gas giant Uranus
with the colder weather it brings.
Warm clothes would then be needed
for planet Neptune too
but they wouldn't be visiting Pluto,
there are far better things to do.

So, all in all, it wasn't too bad
and anyway they could come back,
and getting lost on Mars
took them off the tourist track.
But on the postcards they wrote
to their relatives back home,
they were in total agreement,
next year it's Paris or Rome!

First Shopping Trolley on the Moon

It's what we did with the shopping trolley
that we found adrift in out street,
after we'd played about with it
and rolled it over our feet.

We could have thrown it in the canal,
we could have parked it in someone's yard,
then a voice, I think it was Gary's said,
"Look I know this may well prove hard,

"But I think if we twirl it and twirl it
then hurl it for all we're worth,
just to make sure that gravity
doesn't pull it back down to Earth,

"I think we may well have a first,
the first shopping trolley on the moon."
"You're well off your trolley," we told him,
"You must be some sort of loon."

But eventually we tried it
and watched it rise and rise,
till finally it vanished
and was hidden by cloudy skies.

6

Till the first shopping trolley on the Moon
touched down in Tranquillity
where the Space Police took it away
for being parked where it shouldn't be.

But there's somebody up there now
who's wheeling it around
collecting all the bits and pieces
of space junk that he's found.

And it really is ever so great
and it really is ever so neat
that the first shopping trolley on the Moon
was launched by kids in our street!

Back to School

A week after the holiday begins
and there it is, in every shop window in town,
'Back to School' – I ask you.
As soon as they set us free,
the shops are all telling us
we've got to back again.

I don't want new clothes,
I don't want new pencil cases,
I don't want new maths equipment,
I just want to be left alone.
I want to be on holiday
and not reminded how
in 4 weeks, 5 days, 7 hours,
   39 minutes and 13 seconds
I'll be back at school.

And in one shop they even spelt it
'B-A-K.'
Well I reckon the people who wrote that sign
ought to go back to school too,
so they can learn to spell properly.
And here's what I say
to all those places that tell me
it's 'Back to School' –
"Back off – will you?
It's my holiday!"

The Worst Class in the School

First of all there's my mate Selina,
she makes more noise than a vacuum cleaner,
screams and yells at a very high pitch,
wish we could fit her with an on / off switch.
There's Liam who is far too handy with his fist
and Grace whose knickers are always in a twist.
There's Joe who brings yucky things to school
but his pet tarantula is really cool!
There's Chloe and Zoe who can't sit still
and Michael whose habits make us all feel ill.
There's a quick tempered girl
    whose name is Shannon
who explodes with a ROAR just like a cannon.

There's Shakira and Mira who can't stop yakking
and a kid called Bruce whose senses are lacking,
he really shouldn't be out on the loose,
once he gelled his hair with strawberry mousse!
There's Karen and Sharon who flirt with the boys
and everything Faith does always annoys.
We think she must wash in her mum's perfume
there's a sickly smell all around our room.

poem continues...

There's a lad called Lloyd who thinks it's funny
to hop around and speak like Bugs Bunny.
But nobody laughs, we all think it's sad
and the teachers agree that he must be mad.

Then there's Hannah and Rick
    who go out with each other
and Leroy who's even worse than his brother.
They once brought a pack of soapflakes to school
and emptied it all into our swimming pool!
There's Conan who thinks he's a tough little fighter
and Kelly, when cornered, is known as a biter.
There's Hetty who seems to think she's better
than all of us, so sometimes we get her,
and Felicity threatens to twist her ears,
till we chase her home and it ends in tears.

And there's Malik and Joel, Mohammed and Lee,
Celine, Marisa and finally me.....

We're the worst class in the school
and the worst class RULE......OK?

Learning to Swim

Six weeks to learn to swim.
Six weeks and each time our turn came,
it rained or the wind blew,
whipping up waves on the open pool,
strong enough to sink battleships.
No way that I could stay afloat.
I tried my best but my teacher snarled,
"Fingers away from the edge,
I don't want to say it again."
And if I persisted, his foot
would lay over my hand
like the touch of a butterfly,
till suddenly he'd press down hard
and I'd yell and let go.
And the water would flow
into my mouth and up my nose,
and I'd scream an underwater scream,
then surface, gasp and wheeze,
while all the while it seemed
I'd breathed my last.
He claimed each year that everyone swam
by the time they left his class,
but I beat him...
I didn't.

The Mystery Walk

Tomorrow, Year 6, as part
of your week of activities,
we're going to take you all
on a mystery walk.

Where are we going Sir?

Well, it wouldn't be a mystery
if I told you Barry, would it?

*But my Mum likes to know
where I am Sir.*

Actually I don't know either,
I'm as much in the dark as you are.

*Oh come on Sir. you planned it,
you must know.*

Correction Barry, Mr. Winters planned it.

*Oh well, in that case it will be a mystery.
He can't even find his way to the right classroom
and he's been here twenty years...*

As I was saying, or trying to say,
you will all assemble here tomorrow
at 9 o'clock.

What if it rains Sir?

You'll get wet Barry.
W E T, wet.

poem continues...

But my Mum doesn't like me getting wet Sir,
I catch cold easily,
I'll be off school...

Well, let us all hope for rai...a fine day.
alright Barry, may I continue?

Oh yes Sir. please do Sir.

Make sure year 6 that you bring
a packed lunch...

Salami sandwiches. I love salami sandwiches,
don't you Sir?
Salami sandwiches with mustard, or pickle,
pickle's nice Sir...

I DON'T CARE WHAT YOU BRING BARRY.
YOU CAN BRING A WHOLE STRING
    OF SALAMI SAUSAGES.
HALF A DOZEN WATERMELONS,
A HUNDRED ICED BUNS
AND TEN GALLONS OF FIZZY DRINK,
THEN STUFF YOURSELF SILLY......
NOW JUST BE QUIET AND LET ME
    CONTINUE.

When the coach drops you off
you'll be given an envelope
with instructions for finding your way home.

What if we don't get home before dark Sir?
My Mum...

I know Barry, she doesn't like you being out after dark.

That's right Sir.

Don't worry Barry, we'll find you long before dark.

So you do know where we're going Sir.
I knew it, he does know where we're going,
you can't trust teachers,
they say one thing and mean another.

Have you quite finished Barry?

Yes Sir.

Right, take a walk Barry.

Now Sir?

Right now Barry. And Barry...

Yes Sir.

This time I do know where you're going.

Where's that Sir?

To the Headteacher Barry. I've had enough.

But Sir......my Mum doesn't like me going to the
Headteacher!!!

The Incredible
Mrs. Hulk

She laughs with us, she jokes with us,
she acts just like a big sister,
she's incredible, our teacher,
but we'd really like to meet Mister.

Often she says he's taken her
for a weekend together in Rome
or Paris maybe, or Amsterdam,
he's hardly ever home.

If only he could coach our team
for football on Saturday morning.
but he's out there somewhere saving us all
from some end of the world type warning.

But does he do anything ordinary,
we'd really like to know.
is there some off limits supermarket
where only superheroes go?

So we pester our Mrs. Hulk
for her husband's autograph,
a message perhaps to inspire us
or maybe a photograph.

But he's always talking with presidents,
prime ministers, queens and kings.
He's far too busy she says
to think of such ordinary things.

So we just have to be patient
and pretend it's enough to know
that the teacher teaching us tables
is the wife of a superhero.

And although we know she's incredible
and she acts just like a big sister;
everyone in our class
is still desperate to meet Mister!

Romance

I know there's something going on
between Mr. Phipps and Miss. White.
I've seen them in the car park,
how they linger when they say goodnight.

I caught them once in the TV room
with all of the blinds drawn down.
He said that he'd lost his glasses.
I bet they were fooling around.

When she wafts into our classroom
and catches him by surprise,
nothing is too much trouble,
there's a faraway look in his eyes.

Quite what she sees in him,
none of us really knows:
She's quite fashion conscious,
he wears some terrible clothes.

We think he sends her notes:
Please tick if you really love me,
and if she's slow to reply
we've seen him get awfully angry.

But when they're lovey-dovey,
he's just like a little boy,
cracking jokes and smiling again,
filling our class with his joy.

The School Goalie's Reasons...

(...why each goal shouldn't have been a goal in a match that ended 14:0 to the visiting team.)

1. It wasn't fair. I wasn't ready......
2. Their striker was offside. It was obvious......
3. Phil got in my way, he always gets in my way, he should be dropped...
4. I had something in my eye......
5. I hadn't recovered from the last one that went in, or the one before that......
6. I thought I heard our head teacher calling my name......
7. Somebody exploded a blown up crisp bag behind me......
8. There was a beetle on the pitch, I didn't want to tread on it......
9. Somebody exploded another blown up crisp bag......

10. That girl in Year 5 was smiling at me, I don't like her doing that......

11. The goal posts must have been shifted, they weren't as wide before......

12. I thought I saw a UFO fly over the school......

13. There was a dead ringer for David Beckham watching us, he was spooky......

And goal number 14?
It just wasn't a goal, I'm sorry, it just wasn't a goal and that's that.
O.K?

The Third Team

When I was ten, I was vice-captain
of the third eleven football team.

We spent most of our time
fighting and bickering
and bashing the goalie
if he let something in.

We spent so much time
arguing in the goal mouth
that before we knew it
they were up and at us again.

We were embarrassing,
our teacher used to say,
we always lost by double figures.
He never knew why he bothered with us.

"It's hopeless teaching you lot tactics
or taking you for football practice.
It's a game." he said, "you don't have to try
to maim the other team."

"Just get out on the field and kick the ball,
surely you know enough to do that.
You're just as bad at cricket,
all you want to do is bat!"

But one day we met a team
who were twice as bad as us.
twice as much swearing, twice as much fuss.
Each time their goalie let one through
they changed him over.

Soon we were winning 11-0
and every lad in their team had been in goal.

We were mighty that night,
what a brilliant scoop.
if we'd have been planes
we'd have looped the loop!

We were going places,
we were on our way up.
this week, the third team .
next week - THE CUP!

Baby Paul

When our teacher returned to work,
she came with her new baby.

"A baby shouldn't be any bother." she said.
"I've looked after you lot for months!"

And baby Paul was pretty good -
slept through assembly, dozed during story.

We all kept finding excuses
to take a peep, jiggle the pram.
"Can I wind him Miss?"

It must have been confusing for baby Paul
with one mother and thirty-two minders.
Then once he started smiling,
we were hooked...

We played to an audience of one,
made silly noises,
smiled and laughed, giggled and gurgled,
cooed and tickled.

Even the tough ones
were twisting their faces to strange grimaces,
just to see who could
make Paul smile the longest!

Anyone who forgot their PE gear
had to push baby Paul
round the playground.

Lots of the girls were forgetting theirs
on purpose...
So we made up a rota.

The other kids said we were soppy,
all we'd talk about was Paul.
"You've gone potty," they'd say,
But we were happy, changing nappies.

Other kids had hamsters, goldfish or tadpoles
to look after,
but baby Paul was a big hit
in our class!

Emotionally Scarring

Seeing your teacher
unexpectedly
at a weekend party
can be really embarrassing
both for you
and her,
particularly if she's wearing
a backless top
and looking as if
she's out to enjoy herself.
Even more embarrassing
when you catch her
doing some ancient dance
that no one does
these days -
the twist, the hully gully,
the mashed potato,
the locomotion -
worse than seeing your dad
shaking his limbs in
general disarray.

Then after a formal
hi, hello and fancy
seeing you,
she hides behind
her husband
while you receive
sympathy from friends
who are horrified
at how emotionally
scarred this may
leave you.
Till you realise
what a wonderful
opportunity you'll have
on Monday at
registration
to ask her to show
the class
how she shimmied & jived
to 'Johnny B Goode'

Cold Day at School

Through the open staffroom door, we saw
six teachers, perched three to a radiator
like see-no-evil monkeys, cuddled up tightly
buttock to buttock, huddled together for warmth.
And we wondered why, with such poor circulation,
they didn't take themselves outside,
run around a little,
play chasing games. It couldn't have been because
their clothes were too few, already some
were bundled up like Michelin men.
These teachers were a sorry lot, and we
felt sorry for them, they obviously needed
a kick up the backside to get them re-started.
(and Terry said he'd like to be the one
to kick them!)
But me, I thought they looked ill, looked as if
they'd lost the will to carry on.
And then they noticed us, and if looks could kill
we'd be flat on the floor. "GET OUT," they yelled
and we fled! But next time you pass
the open door of the staffroom, just stay
and take in the view, and think how some day
one of these funny creatures could be you!

It always rains on sports day

It always rains on sports day,
or it has for weeks previously,
and we're sitting there on coats
while the grass is steaming.
They might do better to issue us
with floats, to cope with the dozens of puddles
that punctuate our running track.
And the winner might just as well swim home,
where his winner's rosette will be pinned
to a soggy vest.

It's always fun on sports day,
seeing who gets wettest.
You can bet your life
it won't be the teachers,
they come prepared and swan around
beneath their golf umbrellas,
while everyone else is perched on chairs
sinking deeper into the mud.

29 poem continues...

I hate sports day at our school:
You're out there trying to look cool
in front of parents, brothers, sisters,
grans, granddads, aunts, uncles, cousins,
the lady from two doors down
and your girlfriend from 3C.

And then you slam down in the mud
and you look like a player
in some rugby squad
rather than the bronzed, heroic Greek athlete
that you wanted them to see.

It always rains on sports day,
or it has for weeks previously.

This year it rained so much
that sports day was cancelled.

What a shame!

The Bully

The Bully was always waiting
down the lane by the big tree
or further along at the churchyard gate.

He was someone to steer clear of,
something to avoid, if you could,
like a bad smell from a blocked drain.

He was dangerous,
like a piranha.
One scowl could strip you to the bone.

Most times he wanted sweets,
some days money.
Money made him smile,
money meant you were all right,
safe, for a while.

Once he twisted my arm
so far behind my back
I thought it would snap.

I closed my eyes and screamed inside.
If you let him know it hurt you
he'd do it all the more.

That was when I had no money to give
and I'd eaten my sweets,
but he must have smelt the chocolate
on my breath.

Then the postman came by
and heard the commotion.

"All right lad." he said,
"Let him go."
"That lad's bad." he said.
I didn't need telling that!

The next time no one saved me.
I shouted and waved my free arm
but it HURT, it hurt like mad,
all day and all the next day too.
There had to be something I could do.

    poem continues...

Dad would have said
"Fight your own battles."
Mum was too busy to notice:
"I broke an arm today Mum."
"Oh lovely," she'd say absent-mindedly,
"You must have worked hard."

Robin Hood wouldn't have stood for it.
He'd have rounded up Little John
and Will Scarlet and let the bully have
it.

So I talked to Beryl,
Beryl who helped out
    on dangerous missions
for a packet of salt and vinegar
or a bag of potato sticks.

She said she could fix him.
It would cost of course,
these things always did.
Hit women come expensive.
When he caught me that night

on the road home,
I knew he'd got it coming,
I almost told him.

Next morning Beryl tripped him up
in the mud at the side of the road.
She, and the flying squad she controlled,
ran to school with his trousers.

In the playground, we wound down
the Union Jack that flapped
at the top of our flag pole,
then tied his trousers to the wire
and raised them as high as we could.

When the bully appeared he was crying,
he was actually crying.
and for one brief awful moment
I almost felt sorry for him.

 poem continues...

We wound down his trousers
and handed them back.
He didn't say anything,
just wiped his face
with the flat of his hand
and took them away.

Later that day he found me
in a spot just short of home.
He stood at some distance
and scowled. "Ill get you."
He spat, "I'll make you pay,
if it takes all year.
if it takes......"

"And we'll get you too."
I blurted out.
"We'll pay you back
in a different way."

He spat again.
just missing my feet.
then turned and stomped off
down our street.

Vaccination

When the notes came round
and I read that terrible word,
VACCINATION,
I knew just what to expect.

I'd heard from Ben's brother last year.
how he couldn't move his arm.
He wore it in a sling for weeks,
it went septic where they rammed it in,
came up in a lump - the needle
was huge - like a bicycle pump.

It needed three nurses to hold him down.
He'd been gagged, blindfolded,
while the needle jiggered and jumped around
like a road drill, and all the while he'd howled.

Dad didn't help either -
"In the army," he said, "They lined you up -
thump! thump! thump!
when it got to you
the needle was blunt."

38

"Even navvies and lorry drivers faint,"
some nurse said when I once had
a blood test.

But I'd rather suffer all kinds of diseases,
I'd rather meet with blood-sucking leeches.

And the days tick away, one by one,
as ever closer that BIG NEEDLE comes!

Boys

"Now let that be a lesson," he'd say,
when he gave us three whacks with the slipper.
And for a while it certainly was,
it was brutal medicine
and we weren't too keen to repeat the dose.
The slipper stung and we squeezed eyes tight
to stem any sign of tears.
But memory like pain soon wore off
and we'd mess about again.
Like a badge of dishonour
that we pinned on our chests
we counted up how many times
he'd whacked us.
how many times we'd suffered in silence
afraid to let go a yell.
And there wasn't much pleasure
in a school day with him -
number work, scripture, science. composition,
little variation in the daily routine
and nothing we could do to make him smile.

The girls, of course, came off OK
they were never punished at all,
not even if they did the same as us -
talk when they shouldn't, act stupid,
play the fool, he always kept
his temper with them, never lost his cool.
But boys, they were just an irritation,
to be squashed like insects, their spirits broken,
nasty, foul-mouthed little creatures
who couldn't behave to save their lives.
So as long as he could he would make boys suffer,
it would be his teacher's revenge.

The Wrong Words

We like to sing the wrong words
to Christmas Carols...

*We three kings of Orient are,
One in a taxi, one in a car...*

It drives our music teacher barmy,
his face turns red as a holly berry,
his forehead creases,
his eyes bulge.
It looks as if the top of his head
is about to lift like a saucepan lid
as he boils over...

His anger spills out
in an almighty shout...

"NO." He roars...

"If you do that once more
I'll give you the kind of Christmas gift
you won't forget in a hurry..."

So we sing...
...*most highly flavoured lady...*

"IT'S FAVOURED," he screams.
"NOT FLAVOURED..."

"What do you think she is,
an ice cream cone?"

Then to cap it all,
and drive him really wild
we sing of the shepherds
washing their socks,
till he slams down the piano lid
and takes off like a rocket
into the stratosphere,
lighting up the sky
like a Christmas star.

The Christmas Murder!

Who pulled Sooty's head off?

We needed an answer
when a headless Sooty was discovered
in the debris of Christmas wrapping.

We set up an interview room
and asked everyone the same question:
Where were you when Sooty met his doom?

All the suspects came and went
as we checked their alibis:
Little brother was having a tantrum,
could he have done it
in a fit of pique?
Or sister, playing with Barbies,
was it jealousy?

Both were keeping tight-lipped.

44

We interviewed the turkey
but the bird refused to squawk,
and even though we trod on her tail,
the cat wouldn't squeal.

It was just like Cluedo:
Was it Mum in the kitchen
with the carving knife
or Dad in the lounge
with the rope?

Nobody knew.
There were no clues.

But me, I reckon it was Sweep,
although we couldn't get a squeak
out of him!

Ghost Train

On the g-g-g-g-g-g-g-g-ghost train,
it was dark, it was scary, it was insane,
and I'm never going back there ever again
on the g-g-g-g-g-g-g-g-ghost train.

"It's a lot of fun," my big sister said,
"skeletons, ghosts and a man with his head
tucked under his arm, but you needn't look,
I've been here before." So I sat and I shook

On the g-g-g-g-g-g-g-g-ghost train.

I didn't like it, not one bit,
webs hung down from the ceiling and hit
the side of your face as you travelled past
ever so slowly - oh can't we go fast? –

On the g-g-g-g-g-g-g-g-ghost train.

Coffin lids creaked and a skeleton fell
across our path and I let out a yell
and its echo bounced round the tunnel and back
like a scream from a raving maniac

On the g-g-g-g-g-g-g-g-ghost train.

Back in the open I staggered away.
my sister said. "Maybe another day..."
but no, no way could I ever face
another trip through that terrible place

on the g-g-g-g-g-g-g-g-ghost train,
it was dark, it was scary, it was insane,
and I'm never going back there ever again
on the g-g-g-g-g-g-g-g-ghost train.

47

One Shoe

One shoe by the roadside,
who on earth is careless enough
to lose one shoe?
Surely you'd notice if you hobbled home
on one shoe?
Surely you'd think it was odd?
Some do-gooder would shout out -
"Where's your other shoe then?"
Some busybody would comment -
"That's a strange way to walk!"
You'd be the talk of the town.
one shoe off, one on,
one foot up, one down.
And how could you ever replace
your lost shoe?
Have you ever tried going into a shoe shop
and saying, "I'll just take one please."
Shoes come in pairs, like socks,
you don't find one shoe shops.
So if you're careless and lose one shoe,
best lose the other one too.

Into the Lair
of Baron Jugula

No light ever falls on the bushes and trees,
the flowers there are mostly diseased,
but I went there once for a dare.
I went into the lair of Baron Jugula,
past brambles that tore at my face,
past skulls, picked clean and grinning,
past savage hounds that bayed at my heels,
past the coils of a sleeping three headed snake,
past monstrous eyes and fearsome fangs,
right up to the door of Baron Jugula's Castle
where I stopped and knocked.

And the door swung open to reveal
the bloated, loathsome face
of Baron Jugula.
His breath stank and I shrank back
then remembered why I'd come:
"Can I have my ball back please?"

Shopping Trolley

Scoot down the aisles
in my shopping trolley,
I could go for miles
in my shopping trolley.

Never say excuse me,
never say please,
ram it in the back
of someone's knees.

You really won't
believe your eyes,
my shopping trolley's
been customised.

It's got bull bars,
radio controls,
engine in the back
and it purrs like a Rolls.

It's got a Volvo chassis,
a velvet seat,
and around the store
it can't be beat.

It does somersaults
and big backflips.
roly-polys
and wheely dips.

It does over seventy
miles per hour,
flashing past
in a burst of power.

Scoot down the aisles
in my shopping trolley,
I could go for miles
in my shopping trolley.

Never say excuse me,
never say please,
ram it in the back
of someone's knees

Baby Changing Facilities

It struck me the other day
how strange it was to see a sign
saying - BABY CHANGING FACILITIES.
And this was in a store where
shoppers often bring back clothes
and exchange them for others.
So maybe here they do the same
with babies!
Maybe if your baby screams at night
and you can't stop him,
you'd bring him along to the store
next time you go shopping
and change your baby for another.
Stick him on a shelf and try
another mother's child, take a gamble
on him being less wild.

But really there wouldn't be much of a chance
because all the brought back babies
would be the same.
Maybe baby changing facilities
wouldn't be so hot
if all you got was
another screaming baby when you swapped,
another screaming baby just like the first,
red in the face and about
to burst out of his nappy!

Incident in New York City

The Department of Superheroes
heard a desperate telephone plea.
"Bring needle and thread," a voice demanded,
"And bring them straight here to me."

Then the voice explained what had happened
and how circumstances were dire:
Superman had just torn his tights
on the Empire State Building's spire.

Lost Kitty in New York City

$500 Reward

Nothing has been heard,
not a single word
about the lost kitty
in New York City.
No word from the birds,
it's quite absurd.
The rats won't rat,
the mice said, "Scat,
it's rat-a-tat-tat
if we find that cat."

On Madison Square
she was nowhere.
Up the Empire State
it was too late.
Down on Forty-first
they feared the worst,

     poem continues...

but on Forty-third
somebody heard
that after dark
in Central Park,
three blind mice
spotted her twice,
started a whisper,
a silver whisker
had now been found
on Lennon's ground.

And one of them swore
that the print of a paw
and tracks of blood
had been seen in mud
by the Hudson River —
it would make you
                    shiver......

There's little pity
for any lost kitty
in New York City.

Pie Corbett & Brian Moses, New York City.

Fireflies

(from the observation deck
of the Empire State Building)

The guidebooks all said
the views were stupendous,
the moment, momentous,
the light show tremendous,
but no one mentioned
the fireflies.

But the fireflies
are what I remember the most,
that aerial ballet of tiny sparks
that dipped and danced
and lit up the dark,
that hung a string of fairy-lights
in the sky above Manhattan.

And the light that flamed
from the streets below,
from the beating heart
of this electric city......
I wondered how many fireflies
it took, to stoke up the glow
and keep it burning.

I never expected fireflies
but then, New York's like that.

At the Superheroes Retirement Home

At the Superheroes Retirement Home
nobody rushes to answer the phone.
it won't be a caller in distress
to interrupt their games of chess
or take them away from the television
and send them out on a dangerous mission.
The President never calls to say
"Drop everything. I need you today."
And even the New York City Police
are doing well at keeping the peace.
Now superheroes tend to find
that dominoes occupy the mind.
but Batman likes to play roulette
while Spiderman surfs the internet.

And no one gets out much anymore,
just a trip by boat to the Jersey Shore
to sit in the sun and reminisce
how life was never as cosy as this.
The memories flutter around like birds
as the superheroes, lost for words,
look at each other and silently weep
for one more chase over rooftops,
one last l
                    e
                        a
                            p.

Taxi Tales
– New York City

On a wild ride downtown
the cab driver frowns, tells how much
the city is changing.
"Little shops go," he says,
"Come back as flats.
make big money for someone."
He flicks the wheel,
flings his cab across lanes
like a ball in a pinball machine,
fifty down the avenue at least.
"Hate going through that light,
one night nearly lost my life.
Guy that hit me didn't seem bothered,
jabbered away at his phone.
Gotta go this way though,
it's quickest round Central."

"I do five till five," he says.
"But it's the best job.
Get stressed still
but I'm learning to flow.
Sure. I'm aggressive but who isn't?
It's the other guys who stitch me up.
Hey listen, you should see this place."
he tells me, "Somewhere down on Seventh.
At certain speeds you leave the road.
Don't believe me, do you?
I tell you it's gospel.
four wheels lifted, man, I'm flying.
Somewhere between 17th and Greenwich
see me coming in to land. Sure 'nuff
neater than a plane at JFK!"

America's Gate (Ellis Island)

"I'm bringing something beautiful
to America."   (Girl. 10 years)

If I miss my name
   then I might be forever knocking
      on America's gate.
If I lose my ticket and miss my turn
   I may never learn the lie of this land.
For all that I've planned
   is tied up in this trip.
all that I own
   is packed up in this bag.
And there isn't much money
   but there's gifts I can bring.
And I'm bringing them all to America,
I'm bringing them all from home.
Not my mother's rings
   or my party dress,

not my father's watch
   or my lacy shawl,
just the moon on my shoulder,
   a voice that can sing,
feet that can dance
   and a pipe that I play.
And I'm playing now for America.
   and I'm hoping that someone will notice.
Then perhaps I won't be here forever
knocking on America's gate.

In Any City

There was one who did a dance,
a shuffle of feet across the sidewalk.
There was one with a sign -
"I hate to ask, you hate to give,"
There was one who played drums,
a symphony on saucepans and tins,
while another growled out
"Jumping Jack Flash"
as he strummed a banjo.
There was one humming endlessly,
some sort of mantra.
There was one in a doorway
tented by cardboard.
There was one sifting through debris
with his feet,
while another tenderly lifted cold pizza
from a waste bin.
There was one performing magic tricks
and another arguing with himself.
There was one asking the time
as if time really mattered.

There was one with another sign.
"Why lie - I could use a beer
and a burger"
There was one, there were many,
each with his own Starbucks cup,
hopelessly, hopefully
looking up at us
looking down.

The Snake's Revenge

I'm here, at the edge of your universe,
a creature of immeasurable girth.
Hatred has made me huge, and now
I'm the snake that will swallow the Earth.

And I'm moving ever closer,
I've already gobbled up stars,
I've unhinged my jaws and soon I'll be ready
to take a crack at Mars.

And when I finally reach you
I'll tell you now what I'll do
I shall wrap my coils round your planet
and squeeze the breath out of you.

And this will be my revenge
from the time that I was cursed,
for eternity spent on my belly,
for the dust that I ate, for my thirst.

And remember well, if you will,
for a snake is nobody's friend.
I was there at the very beginning
and I'll be there at the end.

For the world won't finish in flame
or by drowning in a flood.
It won't be wholly engulfed
in an ocean of angry mud.

There'll be no explosion, no fracture,
no tremors from a last earthquake.
I tell you now, this world will end
in the belly of a snake.

All the Things You Can Say to Places in the U.K.

Always say "Ta" to Leamington Spa,
say "Have a nice day" to Whitley Bay.
You can shout "What's new" or even "Howdoo"
to inhabitants of Looe or Crewe.
You can tell the whole story in Tobermory,
say "Hi" to Rye and "Right on" to Brighton.
or call out "Let's go" to Plymouth Ho.
Talk through your dreams in Milton Keynes,
say "it's all for the best" in Haverfordwest.
Always say "Yes" when you visit Skegness
but only say "No" In Llandudno.
Don't tell a lie to the Island of Skye
or say "It smells" in Tunbridge Wells.
Don't talk rude if you're down in Bude
or start to get gabby in Waltham Abbey.
Don't ever plead in Berwick on Tweed
or say "You look ill" to Burgess Hill.
You could lose your voice
    and talk with your hands
when you take a trip to Camber Sands.
but whatever you say just won't impress
the residents of Shoeburyness.

A Big Heap of Romney Marsh Sheep

A big heap of Romney Marsh sheep
are watching the train
as it scuttles by, while I wonder what
a big heap of Romney Marsh sheep
make of this smoking machine
as it snakes through their landscape.
A big heap of Romney Marsh sheep
must be used to this
regular disturbance, but still
a big heap of Romney Marsh sheep
might well prefer some peace and quiet
while they sleep, while they dream,
    and after all
a big heap of Romney Marsh sheep
must have some say if numbers count.
Maybe one day they'll mount a protest
as a big heap of Romney Marsh sheep
stop the train in its tracks,
block the line, wreck the timetable.
A big heap of Romney Marsh sheep
will give no warning!

On the Romney Marsh to Lilliput Line

(Written when I was resident writer on
the Romney, Hythe and Dymchurch
Light Railway in Kent)

On the Romney Marsh to Lilliput line
there are children who like to count
- sheep (thousands), cabbages (millions)
diggers, tractors, haystacks
and lighthouses (only two!)
There are those who yell (LOUDLY)
or sing (tunelessly).
There are dads who tease their kids
with spoooooooooky sounds
in the tunnels,
complainers who whinge about
late trains, lack of space
and those Lowry figures, tall & thin,
folding themselves in two
as they squeeze a way in.

There are jokers who poke fun
at grown men playing trains,
pessimists (frowning)
certain it will rain,
enthusiasts showing off
their Mastermind brains
and their knowledge of
small gauge railways.
And always the ones who've
been here before, aeons ago,
before the war.
All of us waving,
the whole train waving
like so many Gullivers
rolling and rattling, slipping
and swaying, creeping
and cranking
along the tracks and
back down the years
to Lilliput.

Ghosts of the London Underground

In the subway tunnels
  dying to be found,
on the Circle Line
  going round and round,
in the wail of the wind,
  a peculiar sound,
these ghosts
  of the London Underground.

Down, deep down, down deep underground
these ghosts of the London Underground.

And maybe you'll find
  you can see right through
the passenger sitting
  opposite you
or a skull appears
  from beneath a hood,
and you really wish
  you were made of wood,
that you didn't see
  what you think you did
and all these horrors
  were still well hid.

Down, deep down, down deep underground
with ghosts of the London Underground.

No ticket needed.
   you travel free
in the freakiest, scariest
   company.
Stand clear of the doors
   we're about to depart,
so block up your ears
   and hope that your heart
is strong enough
   to survive the ride,
we're taking a trip
   to the other side.

Down, deep down, down deep underground
with ghosts of the London Underground.

And the tunnels echo
   with demonic screams
that chill your blood
   and drill into your dreams.
And you can imagine
   only too well,
how these tunnels might lead you
   STRAIGHT INTO HELL......

     poem continues...

Down, deep down, down deep underground
Down, deep down, down deep underground
Down, deep down, down deep underground
these ghosts of the London Underground.

these ghosts......

these ghosts......

The Stuck-on-the-A1 Party

On a sunny afternoon near Barnsley
we're side by side by side
by side by side
in the biggest traffic jam
since I don't know when,
and the guy in the car next door
leans out and shouts:
"Let's have a stuck-on-the-A1 party!"

So we fetch the picnic baskets
and the bottles of pop.
We get really friendly
and play silly games,
like 'Guess when the traffic
will start up again!'

We play 'Postman's Knock'
and this huge French lorry driver kisses Mum
and looks as if he'd like to do it again
till Dad says, "Watch it chum!"

poem continues...

And a guy in a van selling novelty goods
hands out party hats, balloons
and those things that you blow
to make a rude noise.

And caterers, off to some wedding,
pass round the vol-au-vents
and the chicken drumsticks.
"We'll never make it now," they say.

We swap addresses with people
from the car in front,
"If you're ever up this way again,
look us up..."

And then when a shout comes
to say that we're moving on,
everyone says what a great time they've had,
and couldn't we do it again sometime?

And I'm thinking that maybe
    they'll really catch on,
these A1 parties - they're fun!

Shipbuilding

"You should have seen the ships,"
a taxi driver told me.
"You should have seen the Lagan *
on launch day, the day they first floated
a ship out of Harland and Wolf. **
"I built them," he said. "I played a part,
and proud to know it too,
turning out something so colossal.
Proud to know I'd held the torch
that spat the flame, that welded metal.
It was the same shipyard, you know,
that built the Titanic."
Everyone remembers the ship that sank,
not the successes -
but I'd have been just as proud
if I'd worked on her,
It wasn't the builders who sank her,
they just followed plans.
It was dangerous in the shipyards,
more dangerous than the streets.
A lot of men died, shipbuilding.

"My grandson will never build ships,"
he told me. "He'll never know
the Lagan on launch day.
I still see them though, grand and stately
waiting on the tide.
"My grandson laughs, tells me
I'm daft. "There are no ships granddad.
the yards have gone."
But what was once, never disappears,
that's something the years have shown me.
While the river flows
ships still sail
full steam ahead
to the sea."

* Lagan - the river that flows through
          Belfast
** A famous Belfast shipyard

Fire

There was a fire in our house
when I was a boy,
a living, breathing family fire
that we'd sit in front of,
warming feet or hands
in cold weather.
We'd be blocking the heat
from the rest of the room
till Dad would say, "Let's feel
the warmth." Or if we forgot
to close the door he'd yell,
"Were you born in a barn?"
or, "Put the wood in the hole,
keep the heat in."
It was true what he said,
heat would leave through
an open door,
and even a closed room
would have cold spots,
icy places where you never
felt warm at all.

There were compensations
of course,
in stories by the fire, figures
in the flames, shadows dancing
on the walls, muffins
held against the embers
till they toasted.
Nothing like that these days..
Coming home, coming in from
the street, to be met
by the warmth from radiators
with a cosy and safe sort of heat
that could never fuel
the imagination.

The Bonfire at Barton Point

The bonfire at Barton Point
was a wonderful sight, a spectacular blaze,
stuff legends are made of, wicked, ace!
We were talking about it for days.

There were bee hives, signboards, slats and tables,
car tyres, a sledge and a wrecked go-cart,
a radiogram with a case of records,
some put-together furniture
    that must have pulled apart.

And like patients forsaken in mid operation
there were three piece suites in states of distress,
gashes in sides, stuffing pulled out,
and a huge Swiss roll of a mattress.

And we knew we'd need some giant of a guy
to lord it over a pile like this,
not a wimp in a baby's pushchair
that the flames would quickly dismiss.

But on the great and glorious night
we found it hard to believe our eyes
as tilted and tumbled onto the fire
came a whole procession of guys.

Then adults took over and just to ensure
the pile of guys would really burn,
they doused the heap with paraffin
so no ghost of a guy could return.

Then matches flared, torches were lit
at several points around the fire,
till suddenly everything caught at once
and fingers of flame reached higher.

And beaming guys still peered through smoke
till the fiery serpent wrapped them round
in coils of flame, and they toppled down
to merge with the blazing mound.

With our faces scorched, we turned away,
driven back by waves of heat
till after a time the fire slumped back,
it's appetite replete.

Now as long as we live we'll remember
Barton Point with its fiery display
and the charred and blackened treasures
that we pulled from the ashes next day.

Clacket Lane

(Love Poem for a
Motorway Service Station)

Whenever there's a traffic report
it's you they talk about
Clacket Lane.

Whenever there are queues on the motorway
or a breakdown that's causing a big delay,
it's all down to you
Clacket Lane.

You're the jewel in the ring of the M25,
a place where I can feel truly alive,
I know that I would just drive and drive
to find Clacket Lane.

Your fast food outlets are really fast,
your public toilets cannot be outclassed,
how can anyone ever go speeding past,
Clacket Lane.

You're my pin-up petrol station,
how wonderfully you serve our nation,
the feeling I get is one of elation
at Clacket Lane.

No other service area is quite the same,
I really do thrill to your name,
Clacket Lane,

You have my total admiration,
you're a motorway sensation,
in my humble estimation
you're the best
CLACKET LANE!

The Vindolanda Run

(Vindolanda was a busy Roman fort
close to Hadrian's Wall)

In winter, instead of Roman feet
tramping the iron frost fields,
soldiers slid slalom-like over snow,
riding on upturned shields.

It was wonderful fun, the Romans could think
of nothing that they enjoyed more,
a toboggan run down Cuddy's Crag,
much better than going to war!

And fresh recruits would think it easy
as off on their shields they flew,
till they'd hit a rock and topple off
and the moorland air would turn blue

with Latin oaths and curses they flung
at an unsympathetic sky -
then they'd dust themselves off and climb back up
to the top for another try.

In the ice and snow it was all systems go
for the soldiers patrolling the wall,
they'd challenge each other to see who could travel
the longest without a fall.

Reputations were made or lost
on a run that went really well.
From around the Empire soldiers would beg
for a post at this once northern hell.

And no one thought of war anymore.
Pict hashing had had its day.
The Romans were far too busy
inviting their enemies round to play!

Woad

("All the Britons dye their bodies with
woad, which produces a blue colour, and
this gives them a more terrifying
appearance in battle"......Caesar.)

Let's all go out
and plaster ourselves with woad
(yeah woad!)
frighten everybody silly
as we stomp down the Roman road
(in woad!)

Once we've covered ourselves
with woad,
we'll look twice as ugly
as a warty toad
in woad
(yeah woad!)

We're walking down the Roman road
wearing woad.
Walking down the Roman road
wearing woad.

Woad is great,
woad is cool.
Woad will defeat
the Roman rule.

Woad will help us all
to survive
rushing chariot queues
on the M XXV.

We're walking down the Roman road
wearing woad.
Walking down the Roman road
wearing woad.

Saw ourselves in the lake
and nearly died,
you haven't lived
If you haven't tried
"WOAD!"
(Yeah woad)

*The fashion accessory
of the Iron Age.*

Make Friends
With a Tree

Give a tree a squeeze,
give a tree a hug,
join in celebration
with every bird and bug,

with every bat and badger,
with beetles and with bees,
a new year's resolution,
show kindness to the trees.

Make friends with a tree,
make friends with a tree,
hug a tree, go on show it
you really care, let a tree know it.
Make friends with a tree,
make friends with a tree.

Trees are always homes
to every sort of creature.
In a flat and empty landscape
a tree is a special feature.

Trees can be deciduous,
pine trees are coniferous,
but trees will never hurt you
no tree is carnivorous!

So treat a tree politely,
show it you're sincere.
Long after we have disappeared,
trees will still be here.

Make friends with a tree,
make friends with a tree,
hug a tree, go on show it
you really care, let a tree know it.
Make friends with a tree,
make friends with a tree.

Snuggle up to a sycamore,
cuddle up to a pine
wrap your arms around an oak,
enjoy a joke with a lime.

A tree will always listen,
tell your troubles to a tree.
To the mystery of life
an ash may hold the key.

 poem continues...

So don't be abrupt with a birch,
don't try to needle a pine.
Don't interrupt a horse chestnut,
don't give a tree a hard time.

Make friends with a tree,
make friends with a tree,
hug a tree, go on show it
you really care, let a tree know it.
Make friends with a tree,
make friends with a tree.

A tree is a living thing,
it's not just a lump of wood.
Trees in Sherwood Forest
know all about Robin Hood.

A tree can tell us stories,
a tree knows history,
so in this world of fake and sham
let's celebrate truth in a tree.

Make friends with a tree,
make friends with a tree,
hug a tree, go on show it
you really care, let a tree know it.
Make friends with a tree,
make friends with a tree.

Broccoli

In the place where we stayed on holiday,
there was a painting of broccoli.
And I couldn't understand why anyone
would want to paint
something quite so horrid as broccoli,
something with quite so awful a taste.
What a waste of space,
what a waste of paper.
I bet Picasso was never inspired
to paint broccoli.
Van Gogh had enough trouble with sunsets
and starry nights,
he didn't mess about with broccoli.
And I'm pretty sure that Monet
didn't even grow broccoli
in his garden,
and if he did, he wouldn't have painted it.
Broccoli really is a non-starter.
it doesn't make for great art.
Can you imagine anyone flocking
to a London exhibition of painters
who painted broccoli?
I can't!

Hedgehog Haiku

Droppings on the lawn
left by night-shopping hedgehogs
leaving Slugs 'R' Us.

My Tongue Twister Sister

She's a blister, my sister, my tongue twister sister,
she argues that black is white.
She argues and argues, my tongue twister sister,
she argues with me all night.
She corkscrews my tongue, it's really no fun,
my sister just twists every word,
my tongue twister sister never gives in,
she makes things that I say sound absurd.

She's a blister, my sister, my tongue twister sister,
she is really a blot on my life.
If my sister could only meet Mister Tongue Twister
she'd make him a wonderful wife.
They could argue all night, argue all day
whether something was right or not.
My tongue twister sister
and Mister Tongue Twister
could tie up their tongues in a knot!

This Car

This car has been driven into walls
and into sunsets.
It has slipped down mountain tracks,
almost ending up on its back.
This car has bumped and jolted over fields,
it has heard its own tyres squeal
to negotiate hairpin bends.
This car has almost drowned
in car washes and cloudbursts.
It has clowned around on the road
with crazy young hands at the wheel.
This car has been fingered by thieves
and abused by careless road users.
It has been seen at the scene of crimes.
This car once taxied its way round town,
trekked the motorway network,
rattled noisily through France.
This car, that once was mine,
that died on me,
is now badly beaten and scarred,
on its way to the breaker's yard.

The Cars that Leave our Street

The cars that leave our street
start up in different ways.
Some cough and splutter, then jerk into life,
some tremble and shake, jump forward
then brake, some moan as if
they have bellyache, some shudder and rumble,
some bellow or grumble, some ROAR
with a burst of fire power, some shiver
and cower. Some creep along
as if something's wrong, some leap
with a spurt of speed, some need
the magic touch, the press of a button,
the flick of a switch. Some purr along
without a hitch, smooth operators
shiny and smug, some stubbornly refuse
to break into a chug. Some are well-mannered,
quietly spoken, but one old car.
the one that's ours, despite kicking,
pleading, coaxing, just can't be woken!

Air Guitar

I'm hoping I might get some recognition
if I win the air guitar competition.

I got the most brilliant air guitar.
I found it on e-bay, it'll make me a star.

And it's simple, there's really nothing to it,
in fact any fool can be sure to do it.

This instrument never gives me sore fingers,
it's always in tune when I play.
I never hit any wrong notes,
it's in perfect pitch every day.

Some days it's a Fender,
some days a Telecaster.
Some days it's a Rickenbacker
or a twin necked Stratocaster.

And some days, yes, I'm Clapton,
Jimi Hendrix or Kurt Cobain,
or that guy in a spandex suit,
I just can't remember his name!

 poem continues...

And I'm playing the guitar behind my back,
I'm playing it with my teeth,
I'm playing it upside-down, back to front
and underneath.

And I can make it whine,
I can make it growl,
I can make it hum,
and I can make it howl...

I can play it really loud,
I can play it soft and low,
I can play it so breakneck fast
that my fingers begin to glow.

And I know that every one of you
would like to play like me.
Just hold your invisible axe.
now, are you ready, 1-2-3......

The World's Most Expensive Footballer

The world's most expensive footballer,
has credit cards dripping from his fingertips,
his girlfriend tells of his gold-plated lips,
the studs on his boots have diamond tips.

Euros fall from his trouser pocket,
under floodlights he glows like a rocket,
he's electrical with no need of a socket,
he's the world's most expensive footballer.

He throws paper money to the crowd like confetti,
his finances tangle like a plate of spaghetti,
he's backed an expedition to seek out the Yeti,
he's the world's most expensive footballer.

He dazzles spectators with his fancy passes,
don't stare at him without wearing sunglasses,
all other players his skill surpasses,
he's the world's most expensive footballer.

The Group

There wasn't much to do today
so Malcolm and me and Ian Gray
planned how we might form a group
with me on keyboards, Malcolm on drums
and Ian who knew how to strum a C
and a G on his brother's guitar.

Then Ian's sister came waltzing in
with her friend Sharon & wanted to know
why they couldn't be in the group as well
and when we said no, they threatened to tell
some dreadful secret & Ian turned white,
said they could stay if they kept really quiet.

Then we argued a bit about the name:
"The Werewolves" I said or "The Sewer Rats"
or "The Anti Everything Parents Say"
but Malc said no, it ought to be simple
and Ian said maybe "The group with no name"
while his sister and Sharon said something silly
and Malcolm and I ignored them completely

And I thought we ought to write some songs,
"Easy" we said, "it wouldn't take long
to knock off another *Hold onto your love,*
don't let her go. oh no, no, no!"
And Malc kept the beat with slaps on his knee
while I played kazoo or a paper and comb
till Sharon yawned, got up and went home.

Then Ian's sister and Ian sat down
while we stood around and said what to write,
and it sounded alright till we tried it out
and discovered how awful it was
"Let's knock it on the head," I said
"we'll need another year or two
before we get it right."

And later that night on the short walk home
I said to Malc that I thought we ought
to dump the others and go it alone.
We should have seen it all along,
two good looking dudes like us,
we'd be famous in no time.

But Malc said we were overlooking
one small but very important thing:
Neither of us could sing!

Licking Toads

"What I want to know is this,"
said Sharon. "Is kissing Barry Reynolds
worse than licking toads,
or do they rate about the same
on any top ten list of hates?"
So we did a survey, round
all the girls in our year.
"Would you rather the toad or Barry?"
And everyone had to answer
or Sharon threatened to twist
their arms, but Melissa said
it was cruel to go on about Barry
and we poked fun and said,
"You going to marry him, are you?"
And when we counted the votes
it seemed most girls preferred
to chance the toad
than risk kissing Barry.
Sharon said, "You'd catch less
from the toad." And then we said,
"Let's try again, would you rather
eat a tarantula egg omelette?"
But no one was quite
so sure about that!

Soft Centre

I pull her hair,
call out names,
join in all of
my mates' rough games.

I swagger past
as she looks my way.
strong and silent,
nothing to say.

I mess about,
make out I'm tough,
but underneath
I'm soft enough.

And I'd really like
to hold her tight,
pause for a while
beneath streetlights.

buy her coffee,
talk until late
kiss her goodnight,
tell her she's great.

But I'm meeting my mates
at the club tonight.
I couldn't do it.
it wouldn't be right.

So she smiles
and I scowl,
she speaks
and I growl.

Who's Been Snogging?

(For the Spanish schools I visit)

There's a rumour going round our school
that everyone says is true,
someone was snogging in the library
and it's caused a real hullabaloo.
Someone said it was Claudia
with that boffin we call Harry Potter.
Her face was flushed when they found them
but Potter's was even hotter!
Someone said it was Francesca
with Enrique exploring her charms,
while another bet would be Julia
with Carlos wrapped in her arms
Really it could have been anyone
although there are one or two
who have to be top favourites,
its the sort of thing they would do.
Pablo would snog with anyone
now he and Laura are history,
but no one's been labelled guilty
and the pair are still a mystery.

112

Perhaps it was a competition to find
the longest literary kiss.
was it in the fiction section
where they snatched this moment of bliss?
Or maybe this rumour's a smokescreen
and it wasn't one of us at all.
I bet when they thought they were alone,
two teachers were having a ball,
That hunky drama star Mr. Richards
with ex catwalk model Miss Small!

Kiss Chase

I don't play kiss chase with boys anymore,
they're rough and they're trouble,
they take it too far.
They pester and push and they're rowdy too,
thinking that all they've got to do
Is to corner you somewhere, where nobody sees,
and you'll melt and submit and say,
    "Oh yes please!"
But half of the lads never clean their teeth,
and I don't want to find out what lies beneath
these crumbling rocks that guard their mouths.
so I belt them one, you should hear them howl!
Now they won't play kiss chase with me anymore,
they say I'm too rough and I take it too far.
So all in all it's worked out O.K.
but the odd thing is there's a lad called Ben.
and I really would like to play
kiss chase with him,
but he won't!

No Deal

Becky wouldn't go out with me
unless John went out with her friend Jean.
But John said no way would he never date her,
he'd hated her since nursery school.
I told him that he was really mean
and if he needed help
then I would have shown
what a friend I was.
Couldn't he make an exception I asked,
only once, so Becky could see
Just what she'd miss if she blew the chance
to discover a dude like me?
"I'll pay," I said. "Whatever you want,
and we'll go wherever you like."
But John was determined
he wouldn't give in,
but when I told Becky she said,
"Hard luck, the deal is off
without John."
"You don't know what you're missing,"
I said, but she must have thought
that she did.

I saw her last night with Eric
and Jean was with his friend Mark.
I suppose they come as a package deal,
both of them or not at all,
but I've had it up to here with her,
she's driving me up the wall.
Now John wants to go with Sara
but she won't agree unless her friend Sal
can tag along with me...

I told him to beat it!

Bean Picking

Bean picking one summer with Mike
and two girls I hardly knew.

It was back breaking work
for little cash, but simple.
Even I couldn't make a hash of it.

And Mike was a smooth talker
who rolled from the cradle
bright side up.

He spent most of his time impressing
the girls, I envied his line
in patter, his quick delivery.

I liked to think I might learn
his technique.

And then when it rained we played around
with the girls on the hay in the barn,
all innocent stuff really,
jumping off bales in daredevil stunts.

Till suddenly the playing stopped
and Mike and Brenda paired off,
while Sally was left with me.

I took her hand and we stumbled along
the rows of beans in the rain,
and somewhere in my chest,
in my big kid heart, I felt
the rumblings of first love.

Winklepickers *

Winklepicker shoes weren't fabulous,
winklepickers weren't brill,
winklepickers were the kind of shoes
that made your feet feel ill.

They were shoes that tried to mug you,
when you walked you'd feel them pinch.
They definitely made your feet frown,
brought tears to your eyes, made you flinch.

Both of the shoes ganged up on you,
they made you stumble and trip,
but you kept on putting up with them
because winklepickers were hip.

You knew you looked mean and trendy,
you knew you had fashionable feet
so you made an effort to smile
as you hobbled along the street.

In your Beatle suit and moptop hair
you thought you looked really groovy.
Winklepickers boots could get you noticed,
maybe win you a part in a movie.

And I still remember my winklepickers
and my really embarrassing fate
when I fell at the feet of Valerie Miles
on our first and only date!

* **Winklepickers were very pointed shoes.**

My Life is Over

My life is over tonight for sure
now that Brenda Barnes has sussed me out,
she'll be telling everyone, no doubt,
how I'm really useless at kissing.

Brenda will broadcast it all round school
so I might as well write my farewell note,
join the Foreign Legion, stowaway on a boat,
now I'm labelled useless at kissing.

I practised in front of the mirror for hours,
puckering up and closing my eyes,
but as from tomorrow I'll be in disguise
when the girls know I'm useless at kissing.

Her lips were like fire, I thought I'd been burned,
I jumped back quickly, she obviously thought
I'd rejected her, now my chances are nought,
someone please help me practise my kissing.

I know that I shouldn't contemplate this
but there's no way out, my senses are numb,
overnight, someone please, strike Brenda dumb
and keep secret that terrible kiss.

My Brother's Girl-friend

My brother's girlfriend thinks I'm weird!
I showed her my collection of dead woodlice
and the hairs from dad's beard, but she said,
"Ugh! You're disgusting."

But what I say to her is, "I'm different."
Any kid can collect coins or stamps
but me I'd rather collect
ear wax,
toenail clippings,
squashed spiders
and chewed bubblegum
that's been left under tables.

And anyway,
I don't think there's anything more weird
than someone who *likes* snogging
     my big brother!

Magic Moments

This morning I had
a magic moment
at the supermarket
when the boy
I've fancied all year
reached over to take hold
of the same can of beans
as me.
Our fingers touched
accidentally
and I'm sure he half smiled
and I did too,
nervously.
He almost said something,
he almost asked me out,
I know he did,
but he didn't in the end.
And then yesterday too
I had another magic moment
when this boy who looked
like a rap D.J.
bumped into me in the street.
You should have seen how
he moved his feet as
he danced an apology.

My eyes were pleading
"Ask me out,"
but he didn't.
And these small magic moments
just aren't enough,
I want magic minutes, magic hours,
magic days, weeks, months,
I want magic in my life
BIG TIME,
and I want it NOW!

Freak

Why do I start walking
half in the gutter, half on the kerb,
or wave my arms like a lunatic,
why does everything I say sound absurd?

My voice is always A.W.O.L.
whenever I start to speak,
the words in my mouth are like boulders,
she must think I'm some sort of freak.

Why is it when I take her hand,
mine's all clammy and cold?
She's always calm and confident,
I feel about three years old.

Dad says it's just a phase
and my gawkiness will pass,
but I really do like her a lot,
more than anyone else in our class.

And thinking about it I can't believe
I've any chance of success
when I ask if I can see her again
but she looks at me and says, "Yes!"

Brian Moses writes poetry and picture books for children and resource books for teachers.

For the past 21 years he has toured his poetry and percussion show around schools, libraries and theatres throughout the United Kingdom and abroad.

He has published over 180 books and his poems are regularly featured on CBBC and on BBC radio.

You can find out more about Brian on his website: **www.brianmoses.co.uk**

You can listen to Brian's poetry and percussion at: **www.poetryarchive.org**

Other books by Brian Moses:

The Budgie Likes to Boogie

out now from Caboodle Books

Behind the Staffroom Door: The Very Best of Brian Moses (Macmillan)

Greetings Earthlings: Space poems (with James Carter) (Macmillan)

Taking Out the Tigers - poems by Brian Moses (Macmillan)

The Snake Hotel - picture book (Macmillan)

Trouble at the Dinosaur Café (Puffin Picture Book)

Beetle in the Bathroom (Puffin picture book)

The Secret Lives of Teachers (Macmillan anthology)

There's a Hamster in the Fast Lane - Pet Poems (Macmillan anthology)

Aliens Stole My Underpants (Macmillan anthology)

Walking With My Iguana (Hodder anthology)